T0173725

SAM RIVIERE

Conflicted Copy

faber

First published in 2024
by Faber & Faber Ltd
The Bindery, 51 Hatton Garden
London EC1N 8HN

Typeset by Hamish Ironside
Printed in England by TJ Books Limited, Padstow, Cornwall

A CIP record for this book is available from the British Library

ISBN 978-0-571-38098-5

10 9 8 7 6 5 4 3 2 1

Contents

True PDF 3
True Souls 4
True Mode 5
After Poem 6
Darken Mode 7
Pink Poem 8
Old PDF 9
Old Mode 10
After PDF 11
Safe Souls 12
Safe Colours 13
Safe Poem 14
Dead Dogs 15
True Dogs 16

Dead Colours 17
Pink Fame 18
Old Dogs 19
Dead Mode 20
Darken Colours 21
After Mode 22
Darken Poem 23
Darken Souls 24
Pink Souls 25
Safe Fame 26
After Souls 27
Safe PDF 28
Darken Fame 29
After Colours 30

Dead PDF 31
Darken Dogs 32
Pink Colours 33
Old Colours 34
Pink Mode 35
Old Souls 36
Dead Fame 37
Dead Poem 38
True Poem 39
Pink PDF 40
After Dogs 41
True Fame 42
Safe Dogs 43
Old Fame 45

Acknowledgements

'Darken Souls' / 'Pink PDF' *blush* 2021

'Dead PDF' *Poetry Birmingham* Winter 2021

'Darken Fame' / 'Old Dogs' / 'Safe Poem' *The Poetry Review* Winter 2021

'True Mode' *Times Literary Supplement* 2021

'Dead Poem' *Virtual Oasis* Trickhouse Press 2021

'After Mode' / 'Safe Fame' / 'Darken Poem' *Belfield Literary Review* 2022

'Pink Souls' *Poetry London* Autumn 2022

'After Colours' *The Poetry Review* Autumn 2022

'True Poem' / 'Dead PDF' published as a pamphlet by TEXST (Oslo) 2022

Special thanks to Luca Bevacqua, Melanie Scheiner, Dan Power, Sam Brzeski, Anna Webber, William Kherbek.

This manuscript was composed from December 2020 to January 2021, using Generative Pre-trained Transformer 2 (GPT-2), an open-source neural network created by OpenAI in February 2019.

CONFLICTED COPY

True PDF

A picture-book filled entirely
with text, a soft blue font, white
ink and yellow borders, a simple
grid, a few lines on each page – a
gentle voice, singing as it speaks.

True Souls

Now we finally get into something a little more realistic.
The human imagination can conjure wonderful concepts.
Sometimes I think they actually enjoy it. If that turns into
your job, great. When you put these ideas to work with an
array of props you begin to dream big. Maybe someday it'll
allow your creations (and their customers) to communicate.

True Mode

Now you're done with
the usual paper and ink
(unless this sounds like a
bad idea), you're free to
wander out of the study
room into the open air
and see what's waiting
for you: a view of some
distant city with its
towers looming on the
horizon; some more
mountains to your right;
a vast river flowing
below you in the same
way you just read about
in your notebook.

After Poem by
Thomas S. Powell.
A very good poem
about life in the
suburbs. This one
really reminded
me of my teenage
years. The writer
has a great talent
for conveying
sadness through a
humorous tone,
and making you
want to curl up
into a ball and cry.
The only problem
is that he isn't
quite able to do
that. Some of the
language is a bit
unrefined. Still,
this was a classic.

Darken Mode

I love this. The idea of having a dark environment for kids to work in is very appealing. It takes some of the pressure off them and allows them to relax a bit and enjoy some rest. It will leave you wondering whether maybe they won't work so damn hard at being smart for another four years . . . if it wasn't the first day in camp. I think a bit darker would be cool too.

Pink Poem

A big chunk came from these two poems : (1) the blue ball poem [*http://books.wikimedia*] (2) the pink balloon poem [*http://ebooks.booksac*]. Both I found online. One took about 25 seconds to memorise, while the other was probably a lot more difficult. In any event both of their sections were quite interesting and gave an impression you had to repeat in order to understand. To illustrate they have been rendered in colour and enlarged slightly.

Old PDFs of my other 'children of the 80s'
blog posts are located at [*http://thegreenwallofjoy*]
on Nazism in art. The new print run is available
in hard cover format and is not made in my
lifetime, as I retired earlier this year. Please
contact me with anything specific, or if you just
want something printed out from this particular post.
The current print and PDF set may sell faster
so you might prefer to get this one now.

Old Mode

The only interesting bits are when an element is selected and the next sentence is delivered on top – this means the whole sequence might never end. You know when in music a phrase repeats over two successive bars only, so that you catch it when it's actually ending (and that's a good song)? Here too, both modes offer similar outcomes – one just leaves the sentence without any conclusion, the other does indeed end! That, in itself, is somewhat frustrating.

After PDF generation it is loaded onto my Macbook Pro. As expected there seems no real point in doing this, and only a few words from either side would make an impression in a video of any kind. That leaves the audio of your speech as your last resort. You know this is coming from experience. When my laptop froze a moment after the video ended, and all I was able to hear was random buzzing on speaker, I decided to listen.

Safe Souls

Again I was distracted with these
black and grey arrangements
because I always tend to see them as
more disturbing. I feel it more if I
don't get excited. It seems more
dangerous that if my brain can
actually process everything, all the
good stuff that happens is hidden
beneath it. Perhaps that's why when
I finally do start to see light from the
moon that I know it's time to shut
the shades at last. I want the night to
take a step further than night.

Safe Colours

So why is this particular thing so popular?
First it brings back the feeling of magic
again, which is usually my main reason for
using certain tools. In a recent study, people
who used magic toys reported better
concentration levels as measured by tests
that require them to recall an amount of data
that they already knew. If the memory trick
was effective there ought to be some sort of
measurable effect but what exactly would it
look like? Maybe a change of colour when
you cast your next spell?

Safe Poem

It would not have mattered if his parents could've
seen the face he lived with every morning, how it
was shaped and stretched like an ode to the future, he
would still have smiled through it, like in the picture.
All was clear. The image hung there, as long as he
breathed on it. For years now it had bloomed,
becoming less static, more intricate with age,
growing wider and fainter, changing to a colourless
translucent shade that only made him smile more
slowly, more lovingly, as if in pain from it.

Dead Dogs

The most difficult book to write in a graveyard
is not the one you see when you open your eyes,
not that I would know. I would just like to see
your reaction when the dead dogs start running
down the hall. The story is about a kid who was
sent to a private school, and when he comes
home, he discovers that his parents have all but
forgotten about him. The book is about the way
this family deals with loss. The ending is very
sad, as the ending would have been.

True Dogs

While we could continue this discussion on the symbolism behind the use of animal blood in these designs, the short answer is dogs can be understood to have very complex and subtle emotions. When we consider basic animal needs, a common and fundamental way of relating to humans seems to be that you are just like a dog. You might be shy. Your nose might itch. If things are going horribly you'll bite if necessary. What you really want might not be exactly the same as things you really enjoy doing. Sometimes this isn't an issue.

Dead Colours

It's a rare kind of error – the result of
overthinking the situation – that won't be
noticed immediately; instead there's a
chance that you'll miss the correct message
in the sky, the one you've been watching
for, or the important plot device that you've
neglected to cover up with a single asterisk,
like in a comic, which means its placement
will never register until you look up and
find it in use elsewhere; and all you can do
without any further explanation is wait
while it builds up speed, as a man riding
past with his arm stretched out, ready to
leap when the opportunity comes.

Pink Fame

The Girl with the Broken Pencil is a good novel, but it could have been better. The main character is very well written but she doesn't have much going for her. She does have a pretty good body, though. The problem is that she has a little trouble remembering what she's done. I felt that the author needed more time to focus on what he was trying to say. The protagonist is very similar to my own son, but she isn't the same person. She also doesn't have the same emotional control over her feelings. This is not her fault. It's just how her mind works.

Old Dogs

They had been following the white path which the moon
    had chosen –
for some unknown reason it was the right choice – their
    eyes and voices
followed with strange enthusiasm, their hands were raised
    and fingers
pointing at something in the shadows. They moved slowly
    but as one.
They approached every corner as if in fear, or with some
    other longing,
all eyes fixed onto one spot . . . But after passing there
    was a change, and
their faces turned solemn, their steps faltered. Their long
    bodies sank onto
the ground, their voices lowered, and they started
    whispering a phrase
with terrible bitterness. Their eyes widened until they
    opened themselves
up into empty shells, their hands fell flat, their legs folded,
    and after an
incomprehensible pause their lips moved, but no words
    came out . . .

Dead Mode

He thought at the empty table
in front of the black-glaring
window overlooking London,
the sky still smudged, the
buildings behind the building
he lived in burned, far away as
a cloud might reach. There in
the corner beside him stood a
woman wearing purple
leather. She was not a saint of
course, though she was trying
to help. In his mind he held
still: at any moment she would
be in range again. Her hair
hung low across one side of
her face. The light was the
wrong kind of light. She had
been in that position a dozen
times and it always ended the
same way: the wind blew in
the window, the fire lit her
face as if it held his own gaze
on her, the air smelled like
fresh snow, ancient and cold.
They are here tonight.

Darken Colours

I found myself particularly distracted the whole time
reading both versions since both use a palette of black
colour schemes similar enough to create confusion. In
particular my thoughts wandered towards grey shades
as they often appeared in older editions. My personal
theory is that there are many times in a day, whether
from walking along streets or sitting with old relatives,
that something reminds you of past experiences –
especially memories related to work or family.
Perhaps even more so given the fact the colour palette
used might have more emotional power. And while
you shouldn't be searching for such reminders
for long, you could certainly use it and get better
at it with more exposure. The darker shades of green
on black will probably come naturally to some.
And, since we know that black does indeed represent
darkness, I will say again – use darkness wisely.

After Mode

I have always been impressed by people who manage to maintain relationships beyond the normal bounds of traditional marriage. There seems to be something in us capable of building deep attachments that cannot possibly be sustained even on a permanent physical level. Many years ago someone on reddit wrote something that made me wonder if perhaps the nature of the relationship was actually very complex, because there has always been another side to a person I knew. One that might not be fully revealed. My friend had one more layer of intimacy, but it was invisible to him and that made it that much more painful for us. My question here: if human sexuality cannot be entirely understood because it involves more 'fictional' realities than conventional reality, why shouldn't our 'real world' partners be more mysterious, perhaps like some alien kind of beings that can touch and communicate via telepathy?

Darken Poem

This is the most obvious symptom of a
narcissistic personality disorder – the desire
to create a false persona that is not only
completely different from the real self, but
also causes serious emotional suffering and
damage to the person who believes it.
The same traits are manifested in other
pathological forms of deception, such as
the use of hypnosis to create a false sense of
reality, the creation of fictional characters, or
a fantasy world in which we find ourselves
experiencing our own feelings as a member
of another species – the construction of
elaborate narratives to conceal the fact that
we are not the same person we were before.
Darken the poem and it reveals the exact
reasons for this 'deception', not because it is
some sort of metaphor, but because the poet
himself has never been capable, despite
repeated efforts and promises, of actually
giving me the body I am dreaming of.

Darken Souls

It's all too common to have one's inner voice speak directly to you about another person. In these cases the voice's message is one that could have only originated within our own hearts – it sounds like another's words in your mind, but in fact the underlying thought is entirely a product of your own darkness. In such a situation, when a voice calls to you directly, the first instinct is probably to respond in some fashion, either to reject or to listen, and to go along with the voice. That seems counterintuitive, since the voice was only made to speak directly to you – yet the experience can feel exactly as though you are hearing someone else speaking. What this tells you is that when your heart has gone silent, your sense of self is so removed and distant that even listening can be very difficult. If this is you, please ask the voices if they are aware of this. There should be a definite silence.

Pink Souls

Sometimes all it takes is a small act
of self destruction for the whole
system to be thrown about, like a
giant hand in a puppet show, making
no sense in its own environment, not
trying to hide the existence of its
masters, but showing up in front of
the whole audience, strings twisting
and weaving, a single strand
breaking millions of invisible little
knots that have connected everybody
in a very complex design for many
years . . . It looks to us as if the most
sophisticated set-up in history is at
root a kind of magical joke. What
would appear to the outsider as
random as a dance in a dark cave
turns out to be meticulously
controlled, a ritual which requires
some quite subtle manipulation, and
all the time the audience is kept in
constant tension . . . Even when the
trick is clearly fake, and there
appears to be no hidden message, the
way the ritual is orchestrated is so
elaborate you cannot help wondering
if this is not all part of the illusion.

Safe Fame

It feels so liberating to believe in a world
where this kind of beauty does not exist. I still
dream that my friends have taken refuge in
some other time period. There are moments
when I think to myself this might be the right
way to handle certain issues. When I meet
strangers in unfamiliar locales, I wonder how
safe those thoughts are, etc. In recent months it
has become clear to me that my dream should
be a source of constant vigilance – a refuge
that must exist in a future world that may
already lie in wait. A future where violence
and injustice have been replaced by
compassion and empathy. Where the most
difficult decisions are finally put into the
hands of real people. Where all the dreams that
we have dreamed before fade as you move out
of one building into another. Where beauty is
restored in the places I have been robbed of it.
The words that surround such beauty often
appear terrifying – their presence keeps us safe
in an era that I cannot see beyond.

After Souls

I cannot describe in language how the sound of the wind and
     waves became
like their reflection in ice, when I entered this place. The blue
     sky above us had
long since disappeared from view.

A dream of blue sky was part of this night to me, which did
     not vanish with
each passing morning. Each moment of its memory was
     precious, and too hard
to endure in a world which seemed to contain no time.

Yet I thought to myself in wonder: how could a day long ago,
     on earth, when I
had been waiting with longing for the beginning of life, be
     the last memory I
ever had? And what happened after?

Did death enter us, when an hour would only take a second
     or less – when
the world we had imagined came within range – and with no
     fear, the same old
moment would unfold again?

If we had been able to survive this illusion, we could look
     beyond each other,
as lovers with the same hope for happiness; instead, in each
     other's emptiness,
the dream is broken, and the past begins its cycle in hell . . .

Safe PDF

To use this document as your own (no rights reserved), you need the Adobe Reader which you can get for free in almost any public library . . . Just make sure you can read it with someone watching from a comfortable distance, and remember the rules: don't take off all your clothes before getting into bed; keep the room dark for a day after; don't leave it open in plain view unless absolutely necessary. All that's left is to save your document by placing the mouse cursor inside a closed room where only a trained observer could look – when you put the cursor on an invisible point, a small black space will open above it, then another, and if those spaces overlap (for the reader) there'll seem to be a tiny passage, in which you can scribble any desired hole or curve in space-time that'll advance or slow your reading process accordingly. If the reader notices a gap where two spaces end before joining again, then it's best to close the next room without touching anything in there: otherwise he might mistake it for a 'real' passage leading through empty air.

Darken Fame

When you step behind the curtain that divides you from the
masses of ordinary mortals, you often feel as if something
sinister is going on. This inner space – its inhabitants known
and unseen – has been explored by only a select few, and no
outside source has made the journey to see its wondrous
contents, or even the many hidden chambers that seem to
link it with the rest of the world. Many who travel inside this
realm find they never completely step outside of it, and only
experience the exterior through an increasingly blurred lens,
as they move from one layer to another. If you believe in an
ethereal or at least invisible force behind your experiences,
it is easy to imagine that they were brought to fruition
through direct intervention. The first hint of its existence
might be the sudden drop you felt upon emerging into the
sunlight: the way it cut the air, so that the world itself was
cut in two, separating your view as if by a glass partition.
At the centre however there was no apparent boundary:
an unbroken veil had blown across the air, as thick as rain.

After Colours

As if to remind us that we're not quite alone,
there is a group of mysterious scientists who
seem willing to venture out into that unknown
realm, where nothing is entirely real. What they
find inside their minds is more complicated than
you may initially expect, or perhaps it is a form
you have long dreamt of discovering yourself . . .
Something to do with a hidden dimension and
the existence of strange creatures inside you.
For the time being, the secretists are keeping
this to themselves. In the new light of cosmic
awareness, they may be the first ones to realise
their visions of worlds that are almost beyond
description. For you, the reader of Inner Space,
the mysteries around you aren't yet revealed,
even though they have appeared for a few
seconds during my narration in this very room.
They exist now within you, as though they
always were there. Even today you are an
outsider in your own mind, an observer whose
existence is a reflection of that other presence,
like another star, or something trapped inside a
closed room, that forces it to manifest and
evolve in unpredictable ways – all without
ever revealing its inner nature.

Dead PDF

No more to my name than a small poem,
written on the margins of a newspaper:
'There should be nothing for them to believe
except in dreams'. For now these strange
notes are only known to my sister. I'll try to
recall the story of the cat who got inside the
cellar one summer. A woman was having
trouble sleeping in a neighbouring house and
tried to sneak down to see what the noise
was! She entered through one of the windows
and had an encounter with a strange being.
He called to her with those eyes of his, as
strange as any face that she had ever seen.
She saw him looking with fear into a cellar
window above her head – and she heard him
ask her something. In the afternoon his body
seemed to disappear into the house, as if one
hand were pulling at him while another was
lifting his chin . . . The cellar door had been
closed tightly. The night had been warm and
silent and dark. In the cellar windows light
had not flashed. It would soon take him too;
the next morning the body vanished and no
trace of any human voice was found.

Darken Dogs

In our post-millennial context, the past seems to come alive through its ability to give instant gratification on a cultural scale which has only recently become a fact of everyday life. When that fleeting feeling for something as abstract as the '80s is coupled with an ever-present desire to connect with an ideal version of ourselves, which has all the markings and nuances of our previous incarnations, we might easily mistake those moments as our only opportunity for authentic experience. My personal favourite example: in the '80s I remember my parents driving me to our school in the autumn, which is conveniently the season my first memories of any sort began. I was eight or nine then. We pulled up outside a brick building, it had a roof covered in a thick canopy of leaves from which sunlight filtered down towards a giant sign on the gate. The windows opened on a warm October day and there on the road below glinted the first spark of the new century. My mind could instantly process that image, and with the memory being so vivid it took no more than a few seconds to see how beautiful those words above had been.

Pink Colours

An endless chain of events from here
till infinity, from the moment on whose
forehead our sun glows, to an absolute
void where the glare would vanish;
from the day when the sky above
became blue and purple, to the day that
everything returned to the original
darkness. 'An idea that was never
meant to remain pure: no more colour',
writes Robert Frost. 'But all things
begin as colours, even dreams.' That
line may have escaped with a little
alteration to become more profound,
and we might think of it as a message
written for another era that our own
could not contain, but there we are
again; we're writing for some
generation that may never come
around. Our vision now belongs to an
even further horizon. We live in the
present and its image is not ours. It has
only a vague significance, and when
the sun sets over it, all its colours begin
to burn in a blue haze that covers both
sky and earth, like a single idea that
was not supposed to endure, yet
somehow is real. In this sense we can
call it a dream, a dream that we cannot
escape, but which will last beyond us.

Old Colours

Some people believe a part of themselves, the part that is often called 'the core', can be transmitted from parent to child through the biological connection, usually as a type of psychic or genetic mutation. The connection does sometimes manifest through certain characteristics which appear to indicate the presence of that source within us. When you become sexually active (especially when you are young and inexperienced), you may feel a particular sense of detachment as though your own body and personality may also not be in harmony. Perhaps the physical aspects of intimacy are still too alien for your 'core' to fully understand them, and perhaps what the core doesn't know, and can't comprehend, does become a kind of shadow inside your consciousness, that grows in depth after you have experienced intimacy. A great number of people try to 'balance' or to 'overcome' that connection as if it were another part of themselves, but as a result can lose touch with the inner core completely. The idea that your core is in conflict with your outer self is, in and of itself, an attempt by 'you' to get into another place that makes more direct and immediate 'connection' possible. It seems to happen to people who have suffered traumatic childhoods.

Pink Mode

You remember when I mentioned the black hole that swallows up whole planets like so many little birds? Well there was an article today about one that just disappeared. According to these people all planets come crashing through to the darkness below, and no explanation is so satisfactory as the one they offer up: that the space beneath us is inhabited, but not by creatures capable of intelligent thought. In their theory these beings are trapped because their world is the only place in which they could possibly exist. It could be seen as pretty crazy but this explanation makes a certain kind of sense (maybe). The problem isn't how many civilisations exist around us, but where have all the billions of intelligent beings gone . . . For whatever reason we seem to be the first to reach this point. And these creatures that live within the hollow between the stars may be the key. In other words, a great flood has arrived in the form of some kind of mass extinction, one which has made space that much emptier. Our civilisation isn't at all unlike some kind of dinosaur who has reached this age of relative peace through a series of accidents. The black hole is the ultimate form of natural selection.

Old Souls

The last part of this post should serve as a summary of my feelings about nostalgia as it has changed popular discourse, since those few short years before the phenomenon became ubiquitous throughout the mainstream. What is remarkable and somewhat unsettling in all of this, as someone who spent most of his adolescence obsessed with cartoons, is how quickly we lose ourselves in our collective memories. Like watching children make up names for imaginary friends and playing a game with them, we forget so easily exactly who it was that made up that fictional persona. As farfetched as those stories might seem, my experiences do indeed echo the memories made and sold to us as our cultural inheritance. In an age marked by a hyper-individualistic discourse, that treats the personal as the objectification point for human identity, nostalgia takes on a more universal, transcendent aspect, with our personal histories being reworked like an alchemy process in which cultural artifacts like songs and movies are infused with new elements we would otherwise find meaningless and disposable. I feel that even the most cynical of my generation will have difficulty distinguishing their feelings of longing for that earlier era from their sense of self. Yet this doesn't prevent me from embracing them in whatever light they're offered.

Another interesting note related to blood being shown through the eyes of cats (there's nothing intrinsically strange about that) is the symbolic connection which was suggested back in the 1930s. A famous Italian film that was based entirely around animal experimentation was called Dead Fame. What started life as a more experimental-experimental movie turned into a movie that had a tragic theme, to say the least. It dealt with several deaths due to bad choices and a series of horrific injuries, all of which led up to an inevitable discovery and subsequent cure. A good number of the fatalities were to be expected because of the way that animal experiments were conducted. Animals and humans have evolved from one another. They're designed with a very distinct relationship and understanding of each other, a special type of mental communication between beings that can only come with specific training. This bond has been maintained through all the various scientific advances. And while it may not be exactly as close to what one would associate with magic and paranormal beliefs, these types of connections are just as meaningful. In one form or another human culture relies strongly on animal intelligence and cooperation to complete what's called our human destiny. Animals provide essential assistance to people as a tool of the human imagination.

Dead Poem

I'm not sure if you've heard of the concept yet, or
if it's the most stupid meme that's been created,
but there IS a serious side to the phenomenon of
cyber suicide. If it seems ridiculous and even
sickening and pathetic at first glance, try to
imagine the sheer power those who carry out such
fantasies have, that far eclipses their ability to
ever actually cause anything meaningful in real
life. We all dream about our own deaths and even
in everyday scenarios we have visions of how the
world and society would feel. But the very idea
that someone would attempt to create the ideal
death scenario before actually passing away
makes the most horrific image. In order for the
ultimate goal of such people to ever be realised,
they have to get as close to death as possible, so
the very essence of it seems completely unreal,
like some kind of demented hallucination. Even
on social mediums such as email and instant
messaging there can appear to be little evidence
that a person ever attempted to commit suicide.
Now imagine if your favourite music video ended
up featuring a couple standing behind death
panels, with nothing but balloons and candles for
company, while screaming at the viewer, and then
falling lifelessly to whatever they decided were
their final resting places. That would be a death
that everyone would probably watch.

True Poem

The only real thing I had been looking for while in exile
was a true lyric. I could not find a story to match what I'd
been hearing myself singing in my sleep. My friend said her
father had asked her if her songs had had meaning in his
absence. My life had been shaped too much by my peers at
that age. To me and her, music meant nothing. Nothing at
all. But to them it always seemed an expression that they
shared with one another. They always sang of love, and
sadness, and pain and fear, and joy – even when there was a
little darkness hiding in their voices, something about which
nobody liked to speak. As far as that kind of lyricism goes, I
think there is no room for anything that might disturb the
comfortable circle where people were supposed to belong.
But here a line is drawn. A line which I felt compelled to
cross before I'd heard the music again. If the song was real,
would we care, or notice? Did our words even need to be
sung? This little fragment that escaped to a little ear can
have the same reverberation to us as some very distant
music does. Perhaps all that matters at night is a small
sound echoing across an open landscape. I thought I'd sing
something like this, if the stars had not come out.

Pink PDF

In 2010 an image was posted on the popular image sharing website Flickr with a quote taken from the song 'PDA': 'If the best life comes from pain / I want something to remember I can die'. It was widely reported that this photo had been doctored and turned into an erotic depiction of one of the characters from *Gremlins*. Even though its provenance is not clear, people began creating and uploading similar images for entertainment purposes all across the web. What was particularly interesting about this original image was how little it contained of life after the point of deletion, especially the very brief moment before it was suddenly blown up in a series of digital illusions. Some fans even used the meme's origins for their various forms of artistic performance. And, since the subject would become so deeply embedded in a social landscape often defined by its most bizarre extremes, there seemed little reason it would ever be taken seriously. This all changed in October of 2016 when an anonymous tweet went viral and instantly received worldwide media attention: it was the first time on earth a single word of such massive import was completely stripped of the possibility of ever becoming meaningful. Memeified, then deleted at the same moment its use as an inversion of our traditional culture took effect. That was about three weeks before *Gremlins 3* opened across the United States.

After Dogs

I once got caught reading about the occult when a member
of the choir played an evil sounding brass part at Christmas
service and the church immediately started singing the first
verses of some really obscure hymn backwards. They sang
it while pretending the bass riff was a sinister ghost which
would chase its host out into the desert if she didn't move
in perfect time to match each phrase in reverse harmony for
six straight hours without turning her body towards heaven.
Then another guy tried making light of the occasion using
what appeared to be old footage of Nazi leaders shooting
captured pigeons during World War II in what could be
termed as the very opposite of an act of piety. I asked
where I ought to pay homage to my fellow worshippers
of the devil but I'm afraid it would do my conscience no
credit to say any more because you see the consequences
when my mouth comes close enough to your nose.
Another young woman started taking part by making
a cross with a small wooden rod then putting her leg
behind her shoulder to create friction while bending it
so it resembled a human penis and slowly sliding the head
through her open thighs. All four girls laughed at their
friend until she suddenly had her skirt taken off revealing
her small barely erect clitoris then she bent over the pulpit
and whispered to the assembled audience that no Christian
male would touch or even look at her body whilst it could
be used for her own satisfaction or to please masturbators.

True Fame

I can remember several of my most difficult encounters
(including a serious case involving a guy who literally had
no chance against me) where I just knew I could either get
the fuck out of there, or face a good dose of humiliation.
I'm certainly not an expert in psychological warfare, and it
takes a special kind of mindset on my part to turn on the
aggressor, to be totally ruthless and uncompromising. A
true professional does this with a cool head, a smile and a
certain amount of humour. I guess it doesn't take a master
strategist like John Wayne to understand that if you're facing
an adversary who is doing his or her utmost to do damage to
your ego, you can't take any chances. My friends tell me that
I'm the rarest of rare breeds when it comes to that kind of
situation. As the world goes to shit, no one seems to have
noticed how many good moves they've missed. The real
heroes are those who were lucky enough to witness the
aftermath of major crises. They are not the victims of fame
that Hollywood depicts (and who have become a kind of
cult) and neither should they be considered more important
than the thousands of others who lost their friends and their
careers because some crazy fuck went nuts on the Internet.
In the end, it's just another day in the sun for the 99% who
don't see the real story, the story that's getting played out
over and over until there is no telling where the truth ends
and bullshit begins. This is the real story of the Internet.

Safe Dogs

When a large group of strangers is assembled in
public for the purpose of harassing their respective
family members, it often becomes apparent that a
dangerous atmosphere has established itself. Although
some would say these situations require more
preparation, as a rule they can be resolved very simply
and relatively quickly. A few common methods
include having a 'safe dog' nearby, keeping your car
windows up, having an umbrella ready, locking the
door from the inside and using a flashlight. I often
suggest placing a 'safety zone' around the event
which prevents others from gathering too close. I've
seen situations where this hasn't worked, however,
though no doubt it will come in handy sooner or later,
should you find yourself having any similar
encounters. The key here is knowing when it's time to
use a shield of some type and when to run. If all else
fails, consider using the 'Noise Shield Technique',
but I have my own reasons why that's not always
viable: if the police are still in the area, you may risk
exposing yourself as an 'enemy agent'. In a previous
article I pointed out any noise that might alert an
officer to the presence of a hostile party will also
attract a great deal of suspicion. In most cases I've
seen, even a noise which was innocuous sounding
might trigger a panic. You may find yourself caught
in an extremely stressful situation, surrounded by
enemies of all stripes, trying to escape or fight back,
and the only thought that enters your head is 'The

world must be falling apart around me! And I don't know if I can do anything about it!' And at that moment you're just not really doing your job.

Old Fame

No wonder we have an epidemic disease, with all those former pop singers doing all types of terrible things and having many hundreds of pictures and movies of themselves with the various bodies they would prefer they had. What has never occurred to the mainstream media is that all celebrities go into porn, where every aspect of the human form can be turned to a very positive use. When you have seen the images of celebrities getting their asses eaten there's only one question that occurs to you. Is this some form of medical torture or are they just simply fucking for the fun of it? No one ever said the celebrity life was about pleasure; rather it's supposed to raise you up to an ideal level for the next life. All we can say with certainty is that these images may also be highly addictive. In fact, there are many reports of celebrities becoming addicted to them. The problem is that they have become so accustomed to their own image that they can't get away from it. The result is their personality turns up somewhere far away from the real self that is supposed to drive it, and even the most sophisticated person could find herself slipping into a version of this, just like a new lover who suddenly begins to lose touch with her old life. It's as if the celebrity gets pulled over to another scene or movie, and finds her persona acting without any memory of the previous incarnation; at one point an episode appears that leaves us unable to tell anymore which personality she's projecting into the imaginary body, on whose head floats a star. When we look at this, we can't help but ask ourselves what the difference is between a celebrity and a human being.

Index

After Colours   30
After Dogs   41
After Mode   22
After PDF   11
After Poem   6
After Souls   27
Darken Colours   21
Darken Dogs   32
Darken Fame   29
Darken Mode   7
Darken Poem   23
Darken Souls   24
Dead Colours   17
Dead Dogs   15

Dead Fame   37
Dead Mode   20
Dead PDF   31
Dead Poem   38
Old Colours   34
Old Dogs   19
Old Fame   45
Old Mode   10
Old PDF   9
Old Souls   36
Pink Colours   33
Pink Fame   18
Pink Mode   35
Pink PDF   40

Pink Poem   8
Pink Souls   25
Safe Colours   13
Safe Dogs   43
Safe Fame   26
Safe PDF   28
Safe Poem   14
Safe Souls   12
True Dogs   16
True Fame   42
True Mode   5
True PDF   3
True Poem   39
True Souls   4